AN INSTANT GUIDE TO

MAMMALS

The most familiar species of
North American mammals
described and illustrated in color

Pamela Forey and Cecilia Fitzsimons

BONANZA BOOKS
New York

Distribution map

● Commonly found in these regions

✳ Other species on page also commonly
 found in these regions

○ Partial distribution only

First published 1986 by Bonanza Books,
distributed by Crown Publishers, Inc.

© 1986 Atlantis Publications Ltd.

Printed in Spain

ISBN 0–517–61676–9

CONTENTS

Introduction

The sight of a mammal, like a moose, a sea lion or a chipmunk, gives most people more of a thrill than the sight of any other kind of animal. This is probably because mammals generally are more difficult to find than, for example, birds or butterflies, some are more dangerous and many are less numerous. They are also often shy and tend to come out at dawn or dusk or even to be nocturnal, both factors which make many of them difficult to find. More frequently found are signs that they have been in a particular place in the recent past. Overturned garbage cans in a picnic site at a National Park probably mean that bears visited it that morning, deer tracks may be found in a muddy path or piles of acorns and nuts may be a squirrel's hoard.

This book describes about 140 of the most common species of mammals found in the USA and Canada. Its chief aim is to enable the reader, and newcomer to the study of mammals, to identify positively and as simply as possible, any of the mammals which he is likely to encounter. Tracks and signs are also given, together with the time of day and habitat in which the animals are to be found. Some mammals are much more easy to find than others and these have been described in more detail than those which, although numerous, may be less likely to be seen. Squirrels for instance are active during the day and often seen in wooded back yards; consequently they have been given more space than White-footed mice which are numerous but small and nocturnal and rarely seen.

How to use this book

We have divided the book into eight sections based primarily on the biology of the mammals themselves. The sections are **Primitive Mammals**; **Shrews and Moles**; **Bats**; **Carnivores**; **Rodents**; **Rabbits, Hares and Pikas**; **Even-toed hoofed mammals**; and **Marine Mammals**. Each section is indicated by a different color band at the top of each page. Within each section similar mammals are grouped together as described in the *Guide to Identification*, and each group has its own symbol, so that comparison is made easy. To identify your mammal, first decide to which section your mammal belongs, using the information and symbols in the *Guide to Identification* which follows.

Guide to identification

Page numbers given at the end of each section will enable you to turn directly to the relevant section.

Primitive mammals

Contained within this first section are only two mammals, unrelated to each other or to the other mammals in the book. The first, the Opossum is a "pouched mammal," like those in Australia. Its young are born when very immature and are then carried in a pouch on the mother's belly. It can be recognized by its white face. **14**

The other mammal in this section is the Armadillo which, with its armor plating and jointed appearance, is like no other mammal of North America and is immediately recognizable. **15**

Shrews and Moles

It may seem unlikely that these mammals should be grouped together, since shrews look much more like mice than they do like moles. But these two are both Insectivores — they feed on insects, grubs and worms. They have five toes on both fore and hind feet.

Shrews are small mouse-like animals, smaller than many mice, with soft fur, a long whiskery snout, and tiny, beady eyes. Many of them are quite ferocious, defending themselves vigorously against predators and attacking prey as big as themselves. **16, 17, 20**

Moles are rarely seen since they live underground; often the only evidence of their presence are the mounds or ridges of earth thrown up above ground by their tunnelling operations. They have thick dense fur, some have tiny eyes while others are blind and most have spade-like forelimbs adapted for digging. **18–20**

Bats

The only true flying mammals, these animals are nocturnal. They have small furry bodies, hairless wings and complicated echo location devices in ears or on noses for avoiding obstacles in the dark and for locating insects on the wing. **21–25**

Carnivores

These are traditionally the meat-eating animals, the predators and many of them are hunters and killers. Others prefer a more varied diet of berries and nuts as well as hunting prey animals. A feature that is found in all of them are the big canine or eye teeth and they all have five toes on the front feet; the number of toes on the hind feet may be four or five.

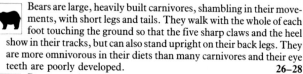

Bears are large, heavily built carnivores, shambling in their movements, with short legs and tails. They walk with the whole of each foot touching the ground so that the five sharp claws and the heel show in their tracks, but can also stand upright on their back legs. They are more omnivorous in their diets than many carnivores and their eye teeth are poorly developed. **26–28**

Raccoons, ringtails and coatis are medium-sized carnivores, with long furry tails and arched backs. They are omnivorous and have poorly developed eye teeth. They are good climbers. **34, 35, 48**

Weasels, badgers, otters and skunks belong to the same family. They vary in size from small to medium-sized carnivores, usually with long slender bodies, short legs, rounded ears and well developed eye teeth. Most are hunters. They have anal scent glands which they use to mark their territories and skunks use them for defence. Some of these animals, like martens and otters, have dense fur, for which they have been hunted. **36–45, 49**

Wolves and foxes are dog-like, with pointed muzzles, pointed ears and long legs. They are effective killers with well developed eye teeth. These animals are the most vocal of the carnivores, making a variety of sounds from howling to whining and snarling. Some are pack animals, while others are solitary. **29–33, 48**

Cats are mostly large carnivores, like larger editions of the domestic cat, with short faces and binocular vision, rounded ears and short soft fur. They have long legs and retractable claws on their feet. They are hunters and killers with powerful, well developed eye teeth. **46, 47**

Rodents

Rodents have characteristic gnawing incisor teeth at the front of the jaws. These are covered with hard enamel on the front surface so that the front of the teeth wears away more slowly than the back, thus ensuring a sharp cutting edge. Rodents have no eye teeth so there is a gap between the incisors and the grinding teeth. Most rodents have four toes on each fore limb and five on the back.

Marmots, ground squirrels, prairie dogs, chipmunks, tree squirrels, antelope squirrels and flying squirrels are medium-sized rodents, many with bushy tails which curl over their backs. All but the flying squirrels are active during the day, so that these animals are amongst the mammals most likely to be seen. Prairie dogs and ground squirrels have a characteristic stance when keeping watch, standing up on their haunches to look around and many have small tails compared to the rest of the squirrels. **50–64**

Pocket gophers, pocket mice and kangaroo rats all have fur-lined cheek pouches opening on the outside of the mouth, in which they carry food. Pocket gophers live underground in long burrows and have clawed forelimbs adapted for burrowing. Pocket mice and kangaroo rats are burrowing, nocturnal, mouse-like animals mostly found in desert areas. **65–67**

True rats, voles and lemmings are small rodents, all sharing certain characteristics of the skull which cannot be seen in the field. Rats and mice generally have short fur, large ears and their long tails are hairless or covered in short hair; voles and lemmings have small ears often almost buried in their long fur and short hairy tails.

68–82, 85

As well as these groups of rodents, there are also other larger animals, like the beaver and porcupine which are unrelated to the other rodents in North America. They all have the characteristic gnawing incisors, which identifies them as rodents. **83, 84, 86**

Rabbits, Hares and Pikas

Like rodents, these mammals have front teeth, the incisors, adapted for gnawing. However they have four incisors in the upper jaw, one pair behind the other and two incisors in the lower. Pikas are small mammals with long soft fur, no tails and large rounded ears. Rabbits and hares are larger with characteristic tuft-like tails, long narrow ears and long back legs. **87–91**

Even-toed hoofed mammals

With the exception of pigs, these large mammals have long legs and hoofed feet with only two functional toes, together forming a cloven hoof. They have horns or antlers. They are herbivores and have a pad of hard cartilage at the front of the jaws for nipping off grasses and other vegetation. The back teeth have complicated crowns and are used for grinding the tough plant food. Included in this group are deer, sheep, goats, buffalo, caribou, and muskox. **92–103**

Pigs have the same two functional toes, but two other toes are present much higher on the leg. They are more heavily built than the rest, with sparse hair and short legs; they do not have horns. Their faces end in disc-like snouts which they use for digging and they have well developed eye teeth which form tusks. **104**

Marine Mammals

The manatee is a herbivorous marine mammal, completely unrelated to any of the others. It is a large, sluggish animal with a thick hide over a thick layer of blubber. It has front flippers, no hind flippers, a broad rounded fluke for a tail and a broad head with thick cleft lips. **105**

Seals, sea lions and walruses have streamlined bodies and front and hind limbs modified to form flippers. They are the only marine mammals which spend part of their time on land (except the sea otter which has been included in the carnivores). **106–111**

Whales as a group includes dolphins, porpoises and whales. They all have streamlined fish-shaped bodies, with front limbs modified into flippers, no hind limbs and a tail which forms a horizontal fluke. **112–121**

Making a positive identification

Once you have decided on the section to which your mammal belongs, you can turn to the pages on which the individual species are described and illustrated. The size of the mammal, from the tip of the head to the base of the tail, is given in the colored band at the top of the page; the length of the tail is then given separately. Four boxes provide information which make positive identification possible. The first box provides details of features or combinations of features which, together with the illustration, enable you to identify your mammal. The second box gives you supplementary information on the biology of the animal. Habitat and distribution are given in the third box and a distribution map is provided for quick reference. Finally the fourth box indicates some of the species with which this mammal might be confused.

Characteristic features

Included in this box is a general indication of the shape and size of the mammal; its fur, color and markings; and any other characteristic features like the shape of its tail or ears, presence of horns, anal scent glands, flippers etc.

Biology of the animal

Included here is the time of day at which this particular species is most likely to be seen; whether it is solitary or lives in groups; and whether it makes a burrow or den. Feeding habits are also given. Many mammals leave signs to indicate their presence, although they may not be seen; such signs include gnawed acorns and pine cones (mice and squirrels) or broken berry patches (bears), as well as scent posts and the remains of prey of carnivores. Where relevant such signs are noted. Tracks are included in the illustration. Also included in this section are comments regarding the protection of the mammal, especially where the species has been subjected to excessive hunting pressure in the past.

Habitat and distribution

There is wide variation in climate and geography in North America, from the mountains and tundra of the far north, to the deserts of the southwest and the temperate woodland of northwest USA. The area and habitat in which any particular mammal is found often provide important clues to its identity. Thus although the Western Gray Squirrel and Eastern Gray Squirrel look very much alike and live in similar woodland, the first is found on the west coast and the second in eastern and central USA. The distribution map will enable you to see at a glance whether any mammal occurs in your part of North America. The third box on each page provides additional information about habitat and distribution; a mammal may not be common, or even present, throughout the whole of its range, being confined to those areas within the range with a suitable habitat.

Similar species

Finally in the fourth box are given some of the mammals with which this one might be confused. Those similar species printed in heavy type are illustrated, either as featured mammals or in the pages of Other Common Species, those printed in ordinary type are not illustrated. Not all related or similar species have been mentioned, some of those omitted may be common in a particular locality.

Other common species

Where relevant, pages of Other Common Species have been included throughout the book. Such a page may form a supplement to a featured species which is one representative of a numerous group, or it may illustrate several less common species which do not merit full feature pages of their own.

Specimen page

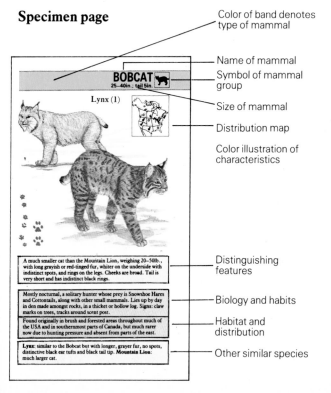

Color of band denotes type of mammal

Name of mammal

Symbol of mammal group

Size of mammal

Distribution map

Color illustration of characteristics

Distinguishing features

Biology and habits

Habitat and distribution

Other similar species

BOBCAT
25–40in.; tail 5in.

Lynx (1)

A much smaller cat than the Mountain Lion, weighing 20–50lb., with long grayish or red-tinged fur, whiter on the underside with indistinct spots, and rings on the legs. Cheeks are broad. Tail is very short and has indistinct black rings.

Mostly nocturnal, a solitary hunter whose prey is Snowshoe Hares and Cottontails, along with other small mammals. Lies up by day in den made amongst rocks, in a thicket or hollow log. Signs: claw marks on trees, tracks around scent post.

Found originally in brush and forested areas throughout much of the USA and in southernmost parts of Canada, but much rarer now due to hunting pressure and absent from parts of the east.

Lynx: similar to the Bobcat but with longer, grayer fur, no spots, distinctive black ear tufts and black tail tip. **Mountain Lion:** much larger cat.

OPOSSUM
15–20in.; tail 10–20in.

The only pouched mammal found in North America. About the size of a cat but in appearance more like a rat, it weighs 8–14lb. It has gray fur, a white pointed face and a long hairless tail. Large hairless ears are black and may have white tips.

Mostly nocturnal and may be seen on roads at night. Female has fur-lined abdominal pouch in which she carries several babies. Feeds on fruit, nuts, roots, insects, eggs and may also scavenge. Can climb trees with aid of prehensile tail.

Found in woodland and farmland in eastern and central USA and also on the Pacific coast. Now found in northern areas where it was previously unknown.

No similar species. May possibly be mistaken for a **Badger**, with its white face, but a Badger's face is black and white. **Rats** are smaller and do not have white faces.

A strange animal, about the size of a cat and weighing 10–15lb., with plates of brownish armor covering its head, body and tail and nine jointed sections in the body armor. It has a soft underside and large soft, upright ears.

Mostly nocturnal and may be seen on roads at night. A good digger, digging for insects on which it feeds, in leaves and earth, and making a large burrow. Signs: burrow entrance is about 8in. across, often made in a bank. Cannot survive frost.

Found in wooded and brush areas, usually near water, where the soil is loose enough for it to make a burrow; in southeastern USA, especially in Florida, Louisiana and Texas.

No similar species.

Dusky Shrew (1)

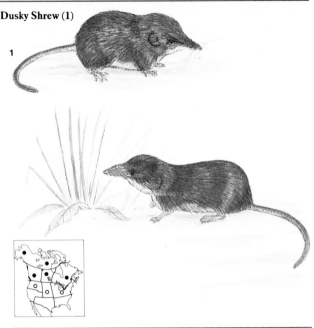

A typical shrew, a tiny animal weighing only one quarter of an ounce, with soft, dense, grayish-brown fur which almost covers the small ears, a long tail and a long snout with sensitive whiskers. Five toes on each foot.

Active at all times, usually searching for food and consumes its own weight in food every day. Feeds on insect grubs, slugs, snails, spiders and worms. Makes a nest of leaves and grass under a log or in dense vegetation.

Found in woods and brush areas where the land is wet, and in marshes and wet grassland throughout Canada except the far north, and in the northern half of the USA.

There are many shrews in N. America. None reach more than 6in. in length. They vary greatly in their distribution but most live in moist places, in woods and near water.

16

Least Shrew (1)

This is the largest North American shrew, weighing up to an ounce. It is gray all over, with soft dense fur and tiny ears and eyes. Its tail is short compared with that of many shrews. One of the most ferocious shrews with a rather poisonous bite.

Active at all times and makes small burrows underground or under the snow. Feeds on worms, insect grubs, snails and slugs which it paralyzes with its poisonous saliva. Makes nest of leaves and grass under log or in dense vegetation.

Found in wooded and brush areas, wet grassland and marshes in eastern and central USA and southeastern Canada, as far west as Nebraska and Saskatchewan.

By contrast the **Least Shrew**, another short-tailed shrew, is one of the smallest. It is distinctively brown in color.

17

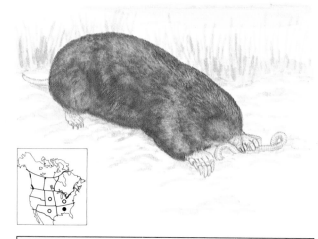

A burrowing animal well adapted for life underground, with broad spade-like front feet which are used for digging through the soil and a naked snout. Eyes tiny and skin-covered, fur is dense and thick, golden-brown or gray in color. Tail hairless.

Active at all times, making an underground burrow, obvious above ground by the ridge of earth thrown up. Feeds on worms and insects found in the course of burrowing.

Found in moist light soil in lawns, meadows and golf courses as well as in natural grassland in eastern and central USA as far west as Nebraska.

Hairytail Mole: has gray fur and a hairy tail. Blind.

A distinctive small mole with many short tentacle-like projections around its nose. It has dense dark brown fur, small but distinct eyes and a hairy tail almost as long as its body. Forelegs large and well adapted for digging.

Active at all times. Burrows can be detected by mounds of wet soil close to water. An excellent swimmer, this mole feeds on aquatic animals as well as catching earthworms underground.

Found in swamps, wet woodland and grassland near water in northeastern USA and southeastern Canada.

No other mole has the distinctive tentacles.

OTHER MOLES & SHREWS

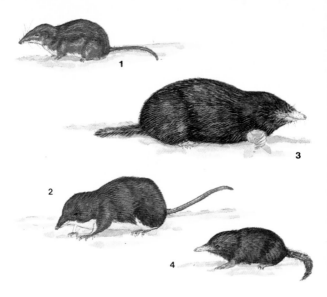

Arctic Shrew (1)
Sometimes called the
Saddleback Shrew, since it has
dark brown fur on its back; its
sides are lighter brown and its
underside is grayish. Lives in
marshes and bogs in much of
Canada, also in north central
USA.

Northern Water Shrew (2)
Large shrew, black above with
lighter underside and very
dense, waterproof fur. Has
fringe of hairs on back feet for
combing out water. Lives in and
near mountain streams and
lakes, in southern Canada and
Rockies.

Hairytail Mole (3)
One of the smaller moles, with
almost black dense fur. Has a
short hairy tail. Ridges of earth
indicate presence of burrows,
lives in the light dry soil of open
woodland and brush. Found in
northeast USA.

Shrew-mole (4)
The smallest of the moles, with
dark gray fur and front feet not
broadly spade-like. It has tiny
eyes, a hairless nose and a long
hairy tail. Lives in the soft moist
soil of coniferous and deciduous
forest of Pacific states.

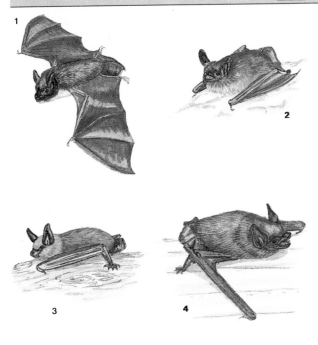

The commonest and most widespread of all the groups of bats in N. America. Small brown bats, with plain noses, ears containing a tragus — a leaflike structure inside the ear concerned with echo location, and scantily hairy tails almost completely inside the membrane forming the back of the wing. These bats generally come out in the evening and are usually colonial, some forming very large colonies. They live in caves, mines, hollow trees or buildings. **Little Brown Myotis** (1) is one of the most common N. American bats, present from Alaska and southern Canada almost to southern USA. Northern populations migrate south in winter to hibernate. **Keen's Myotis** (2) is found in northeast USA and south east Canada; **California Myotis** (3) and **Long-legged Myotis** (4) are both found in western USA and B.C.

Eastern Pipistrel (1), Western Pipistrel (2)

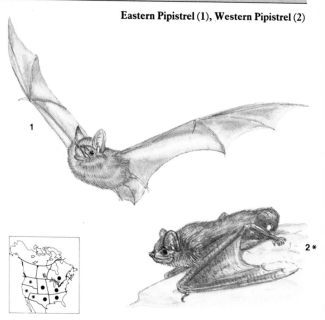

The smallest bats in the USA weighing a quarter of an ounce at most; similar to Myotis bats with plain noses and blunt tragus in the ears. Eastern Pipistrel is reddish-brown. Western Pipistrel is pale yellow-brown and smallest.

Amongst the earliest bats to fly in the evening, sometimes appearing before sunset, with erratic jerky flight. They feed on the wing, taking insects with the aid of the tragues which act as echo location devices. Roost in crevices during day.

Found near water. Western Pipistrel roosts in caves, mines and buildings in southwestern USA. Eastern Pipistrel roosts in trees, buildings and caves in eastern and south central USA.

Myotis bats have longer tragues than the Pipistrels. They are slightly larger and are darker than **Western Pipistrels**.

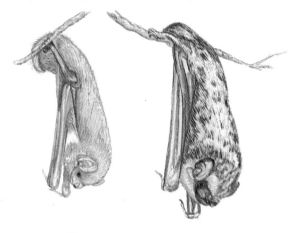

These bats have a frosted appearance due to the white-tipped hairs on the back, furry tails and small ears. Male Red Bats have red or orange fur, females duller red or chestnut fur. Hoary Bats are light brown with very heavily silvered fur.

Both bats live in woodland areas and roost in trees. They fly in the late evening with a faster, steadier flight than the fluttering Pipistrels. Red Bats feed on all kinds of insects but Hoary Bats feed mostly on moths.

Hoary Bats are found throughout the USA and southern Canada. They are not as common as Red Bats which have a similar range but are absent from the Rockies and western Canada.

Silver-haired Bats: dark, almost black fur, about the same size as Red Bats. **Hoary Bats**: larger, the largest bats in the east. Seminole Bats: only slightly frosted.

1

2

Silver-haired Bat (1)
Medium-sized bat (about 2½in. long plus 1½in. tail), with dark, almost black fur tipped with white on the back, small ears and fur on the tail. This is a solitary bat which roosts in the crevices in the bark of trees or in tree holes. It flies in the early evening to feed on mosquitoes and moths. Found in forested areas in southern Canada and USA.

Big Brown Bat (2)
Larger than most bats, (4–5in. long plus 2in. tail), with glossy brown hair on the body, but no hair on the wings or tail, and quite large ears. They roost in small clusters or alone in woodland trees, in buildings or caves and feed mostly on beetles. Can be detected in buildings by their droppings and by marks left on the exterior where they gain access. Found in southern Canada and USA.

Longtongue Bat (1)
Medium-sized bat (2½–3½in.),
with gray or brown fur, tiny tail,
a long slender nose with a
triangular bump on the tip and a
long tongue. The tongue is used
to lap nectar and pollen from
flowers and also fruit juices.
These bats live in caves and
mines in the extreme southwest
corner of the USA.

Mexican Freetail Bat (2)
Smallest freetail bat, (1½–2½in.
plus 1½in. tail), with dense
brown or dark gray fur, long free
tail and wrinkled upper lip.
These bats live in enormous
colonies in caves, like the
Carlsbad Caverns, in southern
USA. They leave the roosts in
huge numbers each night to feed
on insects, returning to the roost
at dawn.

BLACK BEAR
5–6ft.

The smallest of the American bears, standing only 2–3ft. tall at the shoulders and weighing 200–500lb. It varies in color from brown to black but the face remains brown. This bear does not have a shoulder hump.

Mostly nocturnal. Feeds on berries, nuts, eggs, birds, small mammals, insects. Den made in hollow tree or cave. Signs: torn stumps, branches and berry patches, earth disturbed, garbage cans in picnic sites overturned. Valuable game animal.

Originally ranged from northern Canada to Rocky Mountains and Calif., northeast USA and Florida but numbers now much reduced. Common in National Parks in forests and mountains.

Grizzly Bear: larger with distinct shoulder hump, grizzled appearance. **Kodiak Bear**: largest of the bears, up to 1500lb., with shoulder hump, not always with white-tipped hairs.

26

GRIZZLY BEAR
6–7ft.

Kodiak Bear (1)

Large brown or black bear standing about 4ft. tall at shoulders and weighing 300–900lb. Hair is white-tipped, especially on the back, giving it a grizzled appearance. Distinct hump on shoulders.

Mostly nocturnal. Feeds on insect grubs, berries, roots, small mammals and fish. Den made in hollow tree or cave. Signs: torn stumps, berry patches and branches but these last higher than signs of Black Bear, disturbed ground, food caches.

Found in mountain and tundra areas of northwestern Canada and Alaska and in the Rocky Mountains.

Black Bear: smaller without shoulder hump, not grizzled. **Kodiak Bear**: largest of the bears, weighing up to 1500lb., sometimes with white-tipped hairs.

POLAR BEAR
7–8ft.

This unmistakable large bear stands 3–4ft. high at the shoulders and weighs 600–1200lb. It has dense whitish yellow fur. Like other arctic mammals it has fur on the soles of its paws.

A solitary, active, wide-ranging hunter, killing seals on land and at their breathing holes; also feeds on stranded whales, birds, eggs and berries. Signs: seal carcass, snow slide, also Arctic Foxes and gulls may indicate the proximity of a bear.

Found on pack ice, ice floes and on shores along the northern Canadian coasts, in northern Alaska and the Hudson Bay area. A strong swimmer.

No similar species.

A medium-sized animal, similar in size to the Red Fox but with a gray-white coat in summer and a creamy white coat of long fur in winter. The thick coat, fur on the soles of the paws and short ears cut down heat loss in the arctic winter.

Active by day and often follow Polar Bears and scavenge on the remains of their kills, especially in winter. Also take eggs, fledgling birds, lemmings and voles. Den made on a slope, has several entrances about one foot across. Fur valuable.

Found on the tundra of northern Canada, mostly near the coast in winter but moving south in the summer.

Blue Fox: some Arctic Foxes are bluish gray in color instead of the usual white or gray-white.

RED FOX
20–25in.; tail 14–16in.

The most widespread and familiar of the foxes, looking like a
small dog and weighing 10–15lb., with a bushy white-tipped tail,
a reddish coat often mixed with black and a white belly. Legs and
feet black. It has a pointed nose and large ears.

Mostly nocturnal or active in early morning. A hunter catching
smaller mammals and insects, also eats berries. Den on rising
ground, often amongst rocks, has several entrances. Signs: earth
mound at den, buried food caches, bones and feathers.

Found in woodland and more open areas, in farmland and on the
edges of towns throughout much of N. America except for the far
north, the southwest and parts of central USA.

Gray Fox: dark gray in color, has black-tipped tail with black
hairs down center. **Swift Fox** and **Kit Fox** are both rare, much
paler in color and have black-tipped tails.

30

GRAY FOX
20–28in.; tail 10–17in.

Another widespread fox but with a gray coat; the long bushy tail has a black line of stiff hairs down its center and has a black tip. The underside of the animal is rusty red in color. It weighs 7–15lb.

Mostly nocturnal and rarely seen, although its bark may be heard. Feeds on small mammals, birds, eggs, insects and berries. Den made amongst fallen trees or rocks or in hollow log or in burrow. Signs: scent post and buried food caches.

Found in pinewoods or brush, or in chaparral or in rocky areas throughout the USA but not found on the prairies.

Red Fox: reddish in color and has white-tipped tail. **Swift Fox**: buff-yellow back and black-tipped tail. **Kit Fox**: pale gray with black-tipped tail and large ears.

 # COYOTE
30–40in.; tail 10–15in.

A gray or reddish gray animal, weighing up to 50lb., with short hair like a dog. The reddish color is particularly noticeable on ears, legs and feet. It has a pointed nose, and a bushy tail that is held down even when running.

Mostly nocturnal. A scavenger and hunter, feeding on carrion and smaller mammals, but also on berries and worms. Den made underground in burrow or amongst rocks. Signs: intersecting runways with tracks and droppings, yapping at night.

Found in prairies, open woodland and rocky areas throughout much of USA except the southeast, in Alaska and in much of western and northwestern Canada. Common, may be seen in towns.

Gray Wolf: larger and darker in color, tail held higher. **Red Wolf**: rare and only found in Louisiana and Texas, larger than Coyote and darker in color.

GRAY WOLF
40–50in.; tail 10–20in.

Similar to the related Coyote in appearance but larger, weighing 60–120lb. Often darker gray in color, with a broader face. Northern wolves may be white. Bushy tail normally carried horizontally or upright.

Mostly nocturnal. Active wide-ranging hunters living in packs, catching deer and caribou but also smaller mammals and birds. Den underground or amongst rocks. Signs: rest areas and trails marked by scent posts and droppings, howling day or night.

Found in forested and tundra regions of Canada. Very few wolves left now in USA.

Coyote: smaller and lighter in color, with reddish tinge to coat, tail held between legs. **Red Wolf**: found in Louisiana and Texas.

33

RACCOON
16–24in.; tail 8–16in.

A medium-sized animal, weighing 34–45lb., about the size of a dog, with gray fur and a black mask over the eyes, bordered by white fur; alternate black and grayish-yellow rings on the tail which is shorter than the body.

Mainly nocturnal and solitary. Feeds on berries, insects, crayfish, eggs, or may raid garbage cans. Den made in hollow tree or log, or amongst rocks. Signs: den tree may be clawed, crayfish, insect or corn husks, egg shells etc. may be left.

Seen in woodland, open country, campsites and towns, especially near streams, throughout the USA except the Rocky Mountains, and in the very southernmost areas of Canada.

Ringtail: much smaller animal, no eye-mask, white circle around eye instead, tail as long as or longer than the body. **Coati**: smaller animal, long tail indistinctly ringed.

A small relative of the Raccoon, only 2–3lb. in weight, long and slender, with pale gray fur and white circles around eyes; bushy tail has black and white rings and is at least as long as body. Called Miner's Cat since it was used to catch rats in mines.

Nocturnal. Often seen in pairs. Feeds on berries, insects, small mammals and birds. Den made in hollow tree or amongst rocks. A good climber.

Frequents rocky areas and cliffs and chaparral, also woodland, usually near water, in southern and southwestern areas of the USA.

Raccoon: much larger, black eye mask, tail shorter than body.
Coati: long tail with indistinct rings, often held high. Face has no eye rings or mask. Much larger.

MARTEN
14–16in.; tail 10in.

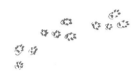

A long agile animal, weighing up to 3lb., with short legs and pointed muzzle, and long bushy tail. Yellowish brown fur with buff-colored throat, tail darker brown. Female smaller than male.

Mostly nocturnal and a good climber. Feeds on squirrels and mice, also eggs, birds, insects and berries. Den made in hollow tree. Hunting for valuable fur (American sable) has led to serious decline in numbers.

Found in woodland usually near water, across Canada except for the far north, and in western USA but not in the mountains.

Fisher: much larger, heavier animal, dark brown all over with no white throat or belly. **Mink**: darker brown and has white chin, feet partly webbed.

Similar in size and appearance to the Marten and weighing up to 3lb., but with smaller ears, a white patch on the chin and partly webbed feet. Fur dark brown, except for chin patch. Female smaller than male.

Mostly nocturnal. Feeds on small mammals, amphibians, fish, crayfish, eggs and birds. Den made in tree or amongst rocks near water bank. Signs: slides in snow like small otter slides and remains of prey. Mink are farmed for their valuable fur.

On the banks of streams, ponds and lakes throughout most of N. America except the southern parts of Florida and the southwest.

River Otter: much larger, with no white chin patch. **Fisher**: much larger, dark brown animal with no white chin patch but with white-tipped hairs all over body.

Least Weasel (1)

A small slim active animal, weighing only up to 6oz., with a dark brown back and white feet and belly in summer; white in winter (when it is called an ermine). Tail is black-tipped. Female smaller than male.

An active carnivore, hunting mostly by night for small mammals and birds on the ground but also climbs trees. Den made in ground burrow, amongst rocks or in tree stump. Shrieks aggressively if cornered or when attacking.

Found in woodland and scrub, usually near water throughout most of Canada and in northern USA except the northern prairies area.

Least Weasel (inset): the smallest weasel and therefore the smallest of the carnivores, tail short with no black tip. **Longtail Weasel**: feet dark in color and tail longer.

Similar to the Shorttail Weasel but weighing up to 12oz., with feet the same color as the back, a longer tail and yellowish-white belly. White in winter (ermine). Tail black-tipped. Southern USA forms may have white face markings.

An active carnivore, hunting mostly by night for small mammals and birds on the ground and in trees. Den made in old abandoned burrow, or amongst rocks or in tree stump. Shrieks like Shorttail Weasel.

Found in a wide variety of habitats but usually near water, throughout most of the USA except the extreme southwest, also in southeast and southwest Canada.

Shorttail Weasel: has white feet and shorter tail. **Least Weasel:** only two thirds the size and much shorter tail has no black tip.

A long agile animal, rather like a large weasel, and weighing 10–25lb., with dense, dark brown fur and a lighter throat. It has small ears and obvious whiskers, webbed feet and a thick, tapering tail.

Usually seen in family groups and active by day. Feeds on fish, also frogs or crayfish. Den made in bank with entrance underwater. Signs: flattened vegetation of resting places, otter slides on bank and scenting posts with droppings.

Found in and around rivers, streams and lakes, originally throughout most of N. America except the extreme southwest, but now absent from much of the midwest.

Mink: much smaller animal. **Beaver**: flat, heavy hairless tail, slower movements.

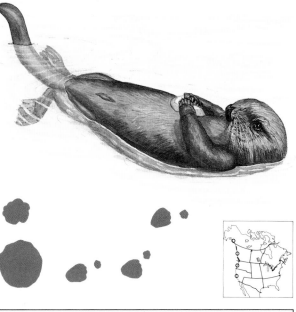

A much larger animal than the River Otter, weighing up to 80lb., with dense glossy, dark brown fur. The hairs have whitish tips. It has a whitish head and chest, flipper-like back feet and small hand-like forefeet.

Lives in groups. Feeds on sea urchins, shellfish and crabs and cracks open these animals on its chest while floating on its back in the sea. The sound of this activity indicates otters nearby.

Found along the Pacific coast, particularly off rocky shores in kelp beds, but now quite rare due to overhunting for its fur. Fully protected.

Seals: have streamlined bodies and fore-flippers instead of hand-like forefeet. **River Otter**: much smaller, lives in fresh water.

WOLVERINE
30in.

A dark brown, heavy-looking animal like a small bear, but with a bushy tail and a broad light brown stripe along each brow and side, and pale spots on throat and chest. It weighs up to 40lb. but the female is slightly smaller than male.

A solitary hunter, wandering over large areas and killing deer, caribou, beaver and smaller mammals. Will also take birds, raid cabins and act as a scavenger. Den made amongst rocks or in thicket. Remains of prey marked with musky scent.

Found in coniferous forests and tundra of Canada and in mountain areas of northern USA.

Fisher: much smaller animal with no stripes on sides. **Marten**: smaller and more slender animal with whitish throat. **Badger**: black and white face, grayish body.

A heavy-looking animal, weighing up to 25lb., with a light grayish body, white cheeks, a white streak on the top of the head and a dark muzzle and brows. There is also a dark spot in front of each ear. Females slightly smaller than males.

Nocturnal. Feeds on small mammals, like gophers and ground squirrels and worms. Signs: den entrance, a hole up to 12in. in diameter, with mound of earth in front. It digs its extensive burrow system with powerful claws on front feet.

Found in open grassland, prairies and arid areas from southwestern and south central Canada to Mexico but absent from southeast and eastern USA and Canada.

Wolverine: found much further north, darker body.

STRIPED SKUNK
13–20in.; tail 7–10in.

A black, long-furred animal weighing up to 15lb., about the size of a cat, with a bushy tail and bold white stripes along each side which meet in a V over the shoulders. When skunk is threatened it sprays a pungent liquid from anal scent gland.

Mostly nocturnal. Feeds on small mammals, insects, eggs and berries and also scavenges. Den made in disused burrow, amongst rocks or under building. Signs: skunk scent and hairs around den, with claw marks in ground.

Found in open woods, scrub and prairies throughout most of the USA and southern Canada.

Spotted Skunk: smaller with white pattern on sides. **Hooded Skunk**: only found in far south of USA. Long tail. **Hognose Skunk**: back and sides are all white.

A small black skunk, weighing up to 2lb., with a bushy, white-tipped tail, white spots on the head and interrupted white stripes on the sides. When threatened this skunk stands on its front feet and sprays scent over its head.

Nocturnal. Feeds on small mammals, insects, eggs and birds and also scavenges. Den made in disused burrow, amongst rocks or under building. Signs: skunk scent.

Found in open woodland, scrub and prairies, usually near water, throughout much of the USA except the northern central area and much of the northeast. Also in B.C.

Striped Skunk: larger with V-shaped white stripe on back.
Hooded Skunk: only found in far south of USA. Long tail.
Hognose Skunk: back, upper sides and tail are all white.

45

MOUNTAIN LION
5–8ft.; tail 2–3ft.

A large brownish yellow cat, weighing 80–250lb., with whitish undersides and a black-tipped tail. The sides of the nose and the backs of the ears are black. It stands about 30in. high at the shoulders.

Mostly nocturnal, a solitary wide-ranging hunter. Kills deer and smaller mammals. Den made in dense thicket or amongst rocks. Signs: food cache covered with branches, scratching posts or urinating stations with piles of leaves.

Found in mountain areas in western and southern USA but formerly much more widespread. Reduction in range and numbers due to widespread extermination.

Bobcat: much smaller, with indistinct spots and short tail. **Lynx**: much smaller, no spots but a black-tipped short tail and large black ear tufts.

Lynx (1)

A much smaller cat than the Mountain Lion, weighing 20–50lb., with long grayish or red-tinged fur, whiter on the underside with indistinct spots, and rings on the legs. Cheeks are broad. Tail is very short and has indistinct black rings.

Mostly nocturnal, a solitary hunter whose prey is Snowshoe Hares and Cottontails, along with other small mammals. Lies up by day in den made amongst rocks, in a thicket or hollow log. Signs: claw marks on trees, tracks around scent post.

Found originally in brush and forested areas throughout much of the USA and in southernmost parts of Canada, but much rarer now due to hunting pressure and absent from parts of the east.

Lynx: similar to the Bobcat but with longer, grayer fur, no spots, distinctive black ear tufts and black tail tip. **Mountain Lion**: much larger cat.

OTHER CARNIVORES

Swift Fox (1)
Similar to Red Fox but with buff-yellow back and whitish underside, large ears and black spot below each eye. Bushy tail has black tip. Now rare. Found in short grass prairies and arid areas in Canada and USA.

Kit Fox (2)
Pale gray fox with whitish underside and black tip to the bushy tail. Very large ears. Found in desert and arid areas with sparse vegetation in southwestern USA, Oregon and Idaho.

Red Wolf (3)
Southeastern wolf with a reddish coat, black in some forms, intermediate in size between Coyote and Gray Wolf. Holds tail upright when running. Found in Louisiana and Texas but now rare.

Coati (4)
Smaller relative of the Raccoon, with thinner brown body, long snout and long tail, indistinctly banded and often held upright. Only found in extreme southern area of USA in mountain forest areas.

OTHER CARNIVORES

Fisher (1)
Similar to Marten but much larger, males weighing up to 12lb. Very dark brown fur (American sable) all over, but 'frosted' with white hairs. Found in forests in southern Canada, northwest and northeast USA.

Black-footed Ferret (2)
Rare animal, (one small population left in Wyoming) which lives in Prairie Dog burrows and preys on them. About the size of a Marten. Fur yellow-brown, but tail-tip and feet black, and face has black mask.

Hooded Skunk (3)
About the size of Striped Skunk but with longer tail. Two forms known, one almost all black with white stripe along each side, other has white back and tail. Found only near streams in far south of USA.

Hognose Skunk (4)
About the size of Striped Skunk but tail twice as long. It has a white back, upper sides and tail, and a pig-like snout. Found in scrub and amongst rocks in Texas, New Mexico and Arizona.

A large, heavy-bodied rodent, weighing 5–10lb., with rather grizzled, reddish or brownish hair on the body, and black feet. Traditionally appears from hibernation on "Groundhog Day," Feb. 2, but this is true only of southern populations.

Mostly active by day. Feeds on green plants like grass and clover and may do damage to crops in farming areas. Signs: extensive burrow system, with one mounded entrance and hole up to 12in. across, and several concealed entrances.

Found in pastures, meadows and farmland as well as in open woodland and brush, in most of southern Canada and in central and northeastern USA.

Yellowbelly Marmot: yellow belly, has different range to south and west of Woodchuck. **Hoary Marmot**: black and white markings on head and shoulders, northern mountain species.

Hoary Marmot (1)

A large, heavy-bodied rodent weighing 5–10lb., with yellow-brown, often grizzled, hair on the back, a yellow belly and whitish patches between the eyes. The feet are light to dark brown, but not black.

Mostly active by day. Feeds on grasses and clovers, may damage alfalfa in farming areas. Signs: burrow with entrance hole about 8in. wide and fan of earth, often beneath rocks or in crevice, usually near boulder which is used as lookout post.

Found in rocky and boulder-strewn areas, in foothills and valleys in western USA and B.C.

Hoary Marmot (inset): found further north, mostly in B.C., Yukon and Alaska, has distinctive black and white markings on head and shoulders. **Woodchuck**: brown, found further east.

PRAIRIE DOGS
11–12in.; tail 2–4in.

Blacktail Prairie Dog (1), Whitetail Prairie Dog (2)

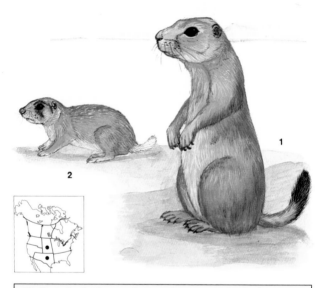

Medium-sized to large rodents, weighing up to 3lb., with yellowish-brown hair, a short tail, small rounded ears and large eyes. They often adopt an upright stance, sitting erect on the mounds at the entrance to their burrows.

Active by day. Feed mostly on grasses. Signs: make extensive "towns" of burrows and mounds at entrances (those of Blacktail Prairie Dog about 1ft. high, of Whitetail Prairie Dog 3ft. high.) Sentries give alert by barking if danger threatens.

Blacktail Prairie Dog is found in short grass prairies throughout western central USA. Whitetail Prairie Dog lives in mountain meadows in western and southwestern USA.

Whitetail Prairie Dogs: smaller, with white-tipped tails and dark patches on face. **Blacktail Prairie Dogs**: black-tipped tails, they make much larger "towns."

GROUND SQUIRRELS

(1) 5½–7in.; tail 2in. (2) 9–10in.; tail 5–6in.

Townsend Ground Squirrel (1), Franklin Ground Squirrel (2)

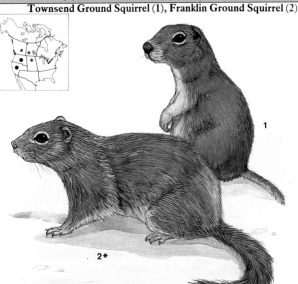

Ground Squirrels are medium-sized rodents. These are two of the larger species. Townsend Ground Squirrel has gray back, whitish sides and undersides. Franklin Ground Squirrel is gray-brown flecked with black, and has a reddish back.

Active by day. Feed on green plants and seeds. Franklin Ground Squirrels also take insects and eggs; live in small colonies; burrow entrances concealed in long grass. Townsend Ground Squirrels colonial; have burrows beneath logs or rocks.

Townsend Ground Squirrels live in sagebrush and grassland in northwest USA. Franklin Ground Squirrels live in long grass and open woods in north central USA and south central Canada.

Columbia Ground Squirrel: reddish feet and legs. Washington Ground Squirrel: smaller and gray with white flecks in coat.
Uinta Chipmunk: short blackish tail.

🐿️ GROUND SQUIRRELS
(1) 10–11in.; tail 7–10in. (2) 9–11in.; tail 5–8in.

Rock Squirrel (1), Calif. Ground Squirrel (2)

Two large Ground Squirrels, weighing up to 2lb. Rock Squirrel is grayish in color, mottled with brown; Calif. Ground Squirrel brown, mottled with white with a dark V-shaped mark between the shoulders. Both have long bushy tails.

Active by day. Feed on green plants, seeds, nuts and insects. Rock Squirrels are solitary and good climbers; make their burrows beneath rocks. Calif. Ground Squirrels are colonial and make their burrows with many entrances on slopes.

Rock Squirrels live in open rocky areas and canyons in southwestern USA. Calif. Ground Squirrels live in open grassland and sparse woodland west of the Rockies in the USA.

Most other similar Ground Squirrels have shorter, less bushy tails. Columbia Ground Squirrel has reddish bushy tail, also reddish undersides and face.

GROUND SQUIRRELS

(1) 4–6½in.; tail 2½–5in. (2) 6–8in.; tail 2½–5in.

13-lined Ground Squirrel (1), Golden-mantled Squirrel (2)

Small Ground Squirrels, weighing 9oz. at most. 13-lined Ground Squirrel has 13 stripes on back and sides, some broken into spots. Golden-mantled Squirrel has golden brown head and shoulders and a white black-bordered stripe down each side.

Active by day. Feed mostly on seeds and insects. Burrows have hidden entrances, those of Golden-mantled Squirrel by a log, rock or tree, those of 13-lined Ground Squirrel under a clump of bushes.

13-lined Ground Squirrels live in southern Canada and central USA wherever the grass is short. Golden-mantled Squirrels are found in wooded mountain areas in western USA and Canada.

These Ground Squirrels are often mistaken for **chipmunks** but chipmunks always have facial stripes as well as body stripes. **Antelope Squirrels** are found in desert areas.

ANTELOPE SQUIRRELS
5½–6½in.; tail 2–4in.

Whitetail Antelope Squirrel

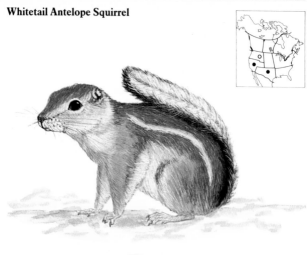

Relatively small rodents, about the size of a chipmunk, with pale brownish-gray backs, white undersides and a white stripe down each side. The long bushy tail is white or flecked white and black on the underside and carried curled over the body.

Active by day. Feed on seeds and fruit as well as insects. Make runways from burrow in ground or rock crevice, but there is no mound at the burrow entrance. These fast-running squirrels run with the tail carried over the back.

Found in arid desert and foothill areas with sparse vegetation, in southwestern and western USA, where they may be seen along the highway.

Whitetail Antelope Squirrel: most widely distributed, with white underside to the tail. Yuma Antelope Squirrel: black and white flecked underside to the tail.

EASTERN CHIPMUNK

5–7in.; tail 4–6in.

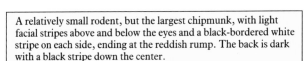

A relatively small rodent, but the largest chipmunk, with light facial stripes above and below the eyes and a black-bordered white stripe on each side, ending at the reddish rump. The back is dark with a black stripe down the center.

Active by day. Feed on nuts, fruits, seeds, roots and insects. Mostly seen on the ground but also climb trees. Extensive burrow made in ground, often on a slope, and with a large food cache, carried to the burrow in cheek pouches.

Found in deciduous woodland and brush in southeastern Canada and in eastern USA, except in the south, and as far west as Kansas.

Western Chipmunks: smaller with four light stripes, not found in east. **Golden-mantled Squirrel:** golden head and shoulders, no facial stripes.

WESTERN CHIPMUNKS
3½–6½in.; tail 3–6in.

Least Chipmunk

Relatively small rodents, weighing up to 4oz., with light facial stripes above and below the eyes and alternating light and dark stripes on the back and sides, four light and five dark.

Active by day. Feed on seeds, nuts, berries and insects. Food is carried to food cache in the burrow in the cheek pouches. They are mostly seen on ground but also climb trees. Burrows are made in ground, often beneath logs or tree stumps.

Found mostly in coniferous woodland and brush, in mountains, in chaparral and sagebrush in western USA. Least Chipmunk is also found in southern Canada from Ontario westwards.

Least Chipmunk: one of the smallest and most widespread.
Eastern Chipmunk: larger with one light stripe on each side.
Antelope and **Ground Squirrels**: no facial stripes.

Cliff Chipmunk (1)
Large chipmunk, with grayish
body and indistinct light and
dark stripes on back and sides.
Feet and underside are creamy
in color. Found in pinon pine
and juniper country and in rocky
areas.

Uinta Chipmunk (2)
Brightly colored, large
chipmunk, with distinct back
and side stripes, and with
reddish fur on its sides and on
the underside of the tail. Found
in coniferous forests and rocky
areas in Colorado, Utah, Arizona
and New Mexico.

Yellow Pine Chipmunk (3)
A brightly colored chipmunk
with distinct back and side
stripes. Its sides and the
underside of the tail are tinged
with yellow. Found in rocky
areas, chaparral and open
coniferous forests in
northwestern areas of the USA
and in B.C.

Merriam's Chipmunk (4)
A large gray-brown chipmunk
with broad indistinct stripes on
back and sides. Found in
chaparral and mixed coniferous
woods in southern California.

Tree squirrels. These two medium-sized rodents weigh up to 8oz. They have reddish-brown bodies, a black line along each side in summer and bushy tails. The underside of Red Squirrel is white; that of Chickaree is grayish or rusty in color.

Active by day. Feed on seeds, nuts and conifer cones. Signs: piles of cone husks and nut shells near feeding stump; loud chattering call. Nest made in fork of tree or in tree hole, made of twigs, leaves and bark; lined with grasses and moss.

Red Squirrels live in all kinds of forests throughout much of Canada, northern USA and in Rockies, often near buildings. Chickarees live in coniferous woods in Pacific states and B.C.

Gray Squirrels: larger, grayer and lack the black lines on the sides. **Fox Squirrel**: even larger with distinctive markings.

GRAY SQUIRRELS

Eastern Gray Squirrel (1), Western Gray Squirrel (2)

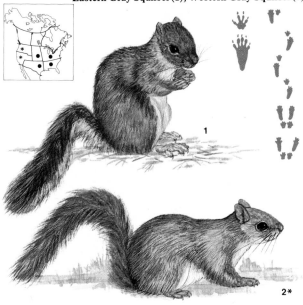

1

2*

Large gray tree squirrels with big bushy tails. Eastern Gray Squirrel has white-tipped hairs on tail, a pale gray underside and a reddish tinge to its fur. Western Gray Squirrel has a white belly, dark feet and white-tipped hairs on its back.

Active by day. Feed on nuts and acorns, Western Gray Squirrel also feeds on conifer cones. Signs: nut shells and cone husks beneath tree, gnawed bark. Large summer nests of leaves and bark high up in tree, winter dens in holes in trees.

Eastern Gray Squirrels are found in eastern USA, as far west as Kansas, in mixed deciduous forests. Western Gray Squirrels live in mixed woodland in the Pacific states.

Arizona Gray Squirrel: found in Arizona and New Mexico. **Red Squirrels**: smaller with red-brown fur. **Fox Squirrel**: larger with distinctive markings.

61

![squirrel icon] TASSEL-EARED SQUIRREL
12in.; tail 8in.

A large tree squirrel, weighing up to 2lb., with distinctively tufted ears, a reddish back and gray sides. It has a white underside to the belly and tail; the upper side of the tail is flecked black and white and bordered with white.

Active by day. Feeds on pine seeds and pinon nuts and the inner bark of the trees. Signs: pine cone husks beneath trees. Nest made high up in tree provides home both winter and summer.

Found in Yellow and Ponderosa pine forests in mountain areas of Arizona, Utah, Colorado and New Mexico.

No other squirrels have such large ear tufts or similar markings. On the north side of the Grand Canyon is a form of this species with a dark underside and an all white tail.

EASTERN FOX SQUIRREL
10–15in.; tail 10–14in.

The largest tree squirrel weighing up to 3lb. It varies in color considerably. The most common color is yellowish-gray with yellowish undersides to tail and belly. Plain gray forms occur in east and darker forms with black faces in southeast.

Active by day. Feeds on acorns and nuts, also on buds and berries. Signs: many nut shells beneath tree used as feeding station. Buries individual nuts for winter. Summer nest made of leaves in fork of tree, winter den in tree hole.

Found in mixed deciduous woods in the north; in mixed and coniferous forests and mangrove swamps in the south, throughout eastern USA as far west as Colorado.

Gray Squirrels: smaller, most are grayer and their coats have white-tipped hairs. **Red Squirrels**: smaller still, reddish-brown and with a black line along the side in summer.

Southern Flying Squirrel

Small squirrels, weighing 6oz. at most, with thick soft fur, brown on the back and white on the undersides. Loose fold of skin along each side of the body, from front leg to hind leg, used to support the squirrel as it glides from tree to tree.

Nocturnal. Feed on seeds, nuts, berries, also on eggs and insects. Nests made in tree holes, especially old woodpecker holes in old stumps.

Flying Squirrels are found in mixed and coniferous woods. Southern Flying Squirrel lives in eastern USA, west to Kansas. Northern Flying Squirrels live in Canada and northern USA.

Northern Flying Squirrel: fur on the underside is white-tipped only, and gray nearer the skin. **Southern Flying Squirrel**: underside fur is all white.

Plains Pocket Gopher

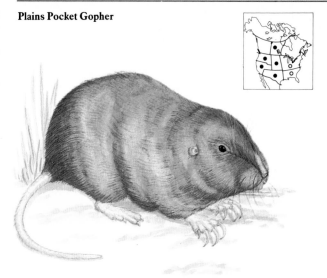

Medium-sized, thickset rodents weighing up to 12oz., densely covered with short hair and with short necks. They have almost hairless tails, fur-lined cheek pouches, exposed orange teeth, small ears and long, curved claws on front feet for digging.

Active at all times. Solitary. They dig burrows, mostly in light soils, feeding on roots and tubers and pulling plants down into the burrow. Food is carried in the cheek pouches and stored in deep burrows. Signs: cores or mounds of earth.

There are many species of Pocket Gophers in N. America, found in a variety of habitats from mountain meadows to prairies and pine woods, mostly in the USA. Their ranges rarely overlap.

Plains Pocket Gopher: lives in prairies, pastures and roadsides in central and southern USA. Northern Pocket Gopher: widespread Canadian species. Other species live in the west.

Hispid Pocket Mouse

Small rodents, weighing up to an ounce, with light brown or gray backs and pale undersides. They have long tails at least as long as the body but not swollen in the middle, short forelegs, moderately long hind legs and fur-lined cheek pouches.

Nocturnal. Feed on seeds and green plants which they carry in their pouches to store underground in the burrow. Signs: tiny burrow entrances, often under a plant and may have piles of earth nearby. Burrow entrance often plugged during the day.

There are many different Pocket Mice found in prairies, plains and desert areas, west of the Mississippi from N. Dakota to Texas and California.

Hispid Pocket Mouse: one of the largest and most widespread, a short grass prairie species. Little Pocket Mouse: small desert species found mainly in Nevada and California.

KANGAROO RATS

4–8in.; tail 5–9in.

Ord Kangaroo Rat (1), Kangaroo Mouse (2)

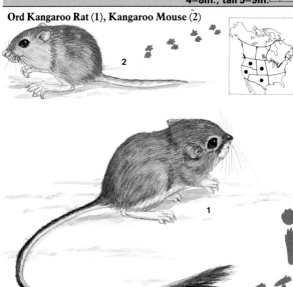

Small rodents, up to 6oz. in weight, with yellow-brown to brown backs, white undersides and black and white markings on face. Tail is longer than body with long tuft of hairs on end section. Very long hind legs make them powerful jumpers.

Nocturnal. Feed on seeds and the green parts of plants when available. Burrow has several entrances, plugged during the day. Signs: burrow entrance often in bank or amongst plants, "dust bowls" where kangaroo rats have been taking dust baths.

Found in desert, chaparral and brush areas; some species also in open deciduous and pine woodland; in southwestern USA.

There are many species of Kangaroo Rats, varying in color, habitat and range. **Kangaroo Mouse** is smaller, with tail swollen in the middle and no tuft of hairs at the end.

Woodland Jumping Mouse (1)

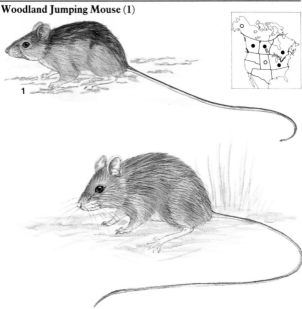

1

Small rodents, weighing up to an ounce, with yellow-brown sides, darker backs and white undersides. They have large hindfeet, very long tails with no white tip, and deeply grooved front teeth.

Mostly nocturnal. Feed on grasses and their seeds, also on fruits and on insects in the spring after hibernation. May jump 3–5ft. in the air if startled. Nest in burrow or beneath log or in dense grasses.

Found in moist fields and meadows, marshes and woodland throughout southern Canada and northeastern USA. Also in parts of northwestern Canada and Alaska.

There are three Meadow Jumping Mice, varying in color and range. **Woodland Jumping Mouse** (inset): orange sides, a brown back and a white-tipped tail. **Pocket Mice**: cheek pouches.

Eastern Woodrat

Medium-sized rodents, weighing up to 20oz., about the size of a brown rat but looking like a large deer mouse. They have long hairy tails a little less than the length of the body, large ears and soft fine grayish or brownish fur.

Nocturnal. Feed on seeds, nuts, acorns, fruits, cactus and green vegetation. Signs: Nest or burrow inside or beneath house built of sticks, stones and bones. Some species make piles of similar materials but not real houses.

Found in variety of habitats from rocks and cliffs to deserts or brush and woodland, mostly in southern and western USA. Most species live in desert or arid areas.

Several species. **Eastern Woodrat** lives in caves in northern part of its range, in burrows in the south. Desert species often make their houses beneath cactus or other plants.

69

RICE RAT
4½–5in.; tail 4–7in.

Relatively small rodent, weighing up to 3oz., with gray-brown fur on the back, paler buff on the underside. It has a long, scaly, sparsely hairy tail, darker in color on the upper surface than the lower, and light gray feet.

Mostly nocturnal. Feeds on water plants, water animals and seeds. May damage crops. Signs: runways and feeding platforms of bent grass in marshes. Grass fragments, crab shells and droppings. Nest of woven grass in clump of vegetation.

Found in marshy areas and amongst grasses and sedges on their margins in southeastern USA and northwards to New Jersey.

Cotton Rats: larger with relatively shorter, hairier tails. **Brown** and **Black Rats**: larger still with dark undersides. **Woodrats**: white undersides.

Hispid Cotton Rat

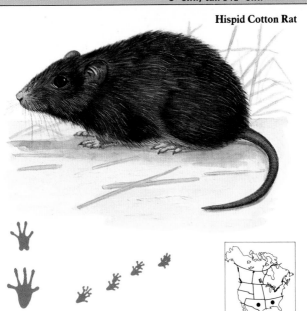

Medium-sized rodents, like a brown rat, but with dark grayish or brownish, coarse grizzled fur. The short-haired tails are shorter than the body and much darker on the upper surface than on the lower. Ears are almost hidden in the fur.

Mostly nocturnal. Feed on green vegetation and may damage crops like alfalfa, sweet potatoes or sugar cane. Signs: trails in long grass and nests of grass, either above ground or in burrows.

Found in grassland and fields in southern USA.

Hispid Cotton Rat: most common and most widespread. Yellownose Cotton Rat: a foothills species living in dense vegetation.

71

BROWN AND BLACK RATS
7–10in.; tail 5–10in.

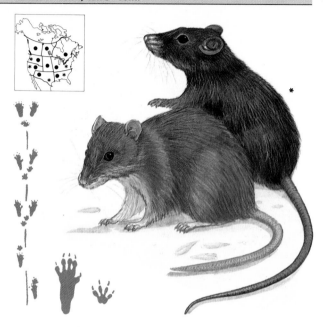

Medium-sized rodents, weighing 5–10oz., with long scaly tails.
Both have gray-brown fur with only slightly lighter undersides.
Tail is shorter than body in Brown Rat, longer than body in Black
Rat. Introduced from Europe.

Mostly nocturnal. Feed on grain, meat, stores and wild plants.
Signs: gnawed food and furnishings, runways from food to
burrow, droppings. They make burrows and tunnels beneath
boards, in walls and in the ground, also in garbage tips.

Brown Rats are found in cities, around farms and in cultivated
land throughout N. America. Black Rats are most common in
cities and on waterfronts in southern USA and up the coasts.

Woodrats: white undersides. **Rice Rats**: smaller, and the fur on
the back is darker than on the underside. **Cotton Rats**: shorter,
hairier tails.

A small dark gray rodent, weighing up to an ounce, with quite large ears and a long hairless tail as long as or longer than the body and dark in color.

Nocturnal. Feeds on anything edible, grain, bread, stores etc. Signs: gnawed food in cupboards, droppings, shredded newspapers for bedding. Breeds very quickly throughout the year.

Found in buildings and cultivated fields throughout the USA and southern Canada. A European mouse which has spread through the continent with man since the sixteenth century.

Harvest Mice: mostly smaller and browner with paler undersides and grooved front teeth. **White-footed Mice**: white undersides and feet.

73

HARVEST MICE
2–3in.; tail 1½–4in.

Western Harvest Mouse

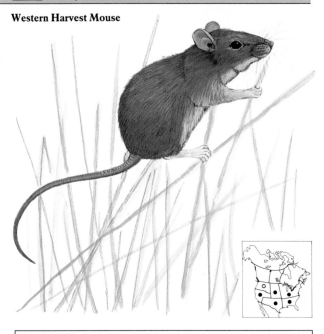

Small rodents, weighing an ounce at most, with brown or gray backs and somewhat lighter undersides varying with species, quite large ears and long tails. There is a groove on the front teeth.

Nocturnal. Feed on seeds and the young parts of green plants. Signs: nest made of grass about the size of an orange, suspended above the ground in surrounding vegetation. Desert animals may live in burrow.

Found in a variety of habitats depending on species, from dry grassland and desert to wet meadows and saltmarshes, throughout most of the USA.

Western Harvest Mouse: most widely distributed, living in grassland and desert throughout much of the USA. Eastern Harvest Mouse: lives in meadows in southeastern USA.

GRASSHOPPER MICE
3½–5in.; tail 1–2in.

Northern Grasshopper Mouse

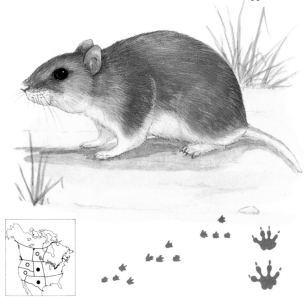

Small rodents, weighing about an ounce, with either grayish or brownish-pink backs and white undersides. They are relatively heavy-bodied, with short white-tipped tails and quite large ears.

Nocturnal. Feed on grasshoppers, scorpions, other mice, nuts and seeds. Northern Grasshopper Mouse makes large burrow with cache points, nesting site and escape burrows. Southern Grasshopper Mouse may live in burrow of gopher or ground squirrel.

Northern Grasshopper Mouse found in deserts and prairies in central and southern USA. Southern Grasshopper Mouse only found in deserts of southwestern USA.

Short tail and heavy body of Grasshopper Mice distinguishes them from **White-footed Mice**. The **Northern Grasshopper Mouse** is larger than the Southern.

75

WHITE-FOOTED MICE
3½–4½in.; tail 2½–4½in.

White-footed Mouse

Small rodents, weighing up to 1½oz., with brown or reddish-brown hair on their backs, white undersides and feet, large ears and long tails often as long as the body.

Nocturnal. Feed on seeds, nuts, acorns and berries as well as insects. Signs: nest made in old bird's nest or in burrow in stump, log, rock crevice, under building etc. Nest or log may contain food cache of nuts and seeds.

Found in many different habitats from dry woodland and forested areas to rocks and chaparral, wet woods and marshes, throughout the USA.

The White-footed Mouse lives in woods in eastern USA. It is one of several mice, often known collectively as White-footed Mice which include Brush Mice, Pinon Mice and **Deer Mice**.

Probably the most common and widespread mammal in North America; one of the smallest of the White-footed Mice. There are two forms, a woodland form and a prairie form, the second being the smaller of the two. Tail dark above, white below.

Nocturnal. Feeds on seeds, nuts and acorns or on prairie grass seeds. Signs: small burrow in the ground or in a stump, log or building, with food cache of nuts and seeds.

Found in dry open woods, grassland and prairies throughout the USA and much of Canada.

Not easy to distinguish from other **White-footed Mice** but its small size, relatively smaller ears and the two colors of the tail distinguish it from many of them.

BOG LEMMINGS
3½–4½in.; tail about 1in.

Southern Bog Lemming

Small rodents, weighing about an ounce, with long soft fur, brown on the back and light gray or silvery on the underside. They have very short tails, small ears almost hidden in the fur and small eyes. Their upper front teeth are grooved.

Active during both day and night. Feed on grasses, clovers and sedges. Signs: burrows and runways at base of the vegetation, woven grass nest above ground or in burrows. Grass fragments and green droppings.

Southern Bog Lemming found in grassy meadows and bogs in northern and northeastern USA, southeast Canada. Northern Bog Lemming found on tundra, alpine meadows in northern Canada.

Brown Lemming: red-brown back. **Collared Lemming**; dark stripe on back. **Voles**: longer tails and brownish fur.

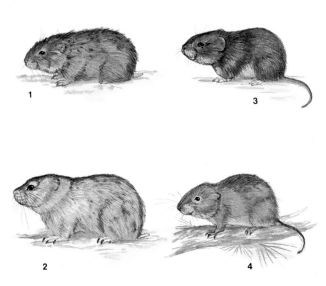

Brown Lemming (1)
Small rodent with chestnut red-brown fur on the back, grayish head and undersides. Ears small and buried in fur, eyes small. Tail short and thick. Lives in tundra and meadows in north-west Canada.

Collared Lemming (2)
Small rodent with light buff-gray fur and a black stripe along the center of the back. Pale yellowish stripe around throat, the "collar". Turn white in winter. Found in northwest Canada.

Mountain Phenacomys (3)
Small rodent with grayish-brown grizzled back, light gray underside and white feet. Lives in mountain areas amongst blueberries and heather in Canada and northwest USA.

Tree Phenacomys (4)
Small rodent with bright red-brown back and whitish underside. Live in large nests made of twigs and fir needles in Douglas Fir trees in coastal areas of Oregon and California.

REDBACK VOLES
3½–4½in.; tail 1–2in.

Southern Redback Vole

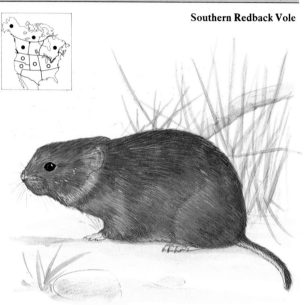

Small rodents, weighing up to an ounce, with long soft fur, red-brown on back, light gray on underside and often yellowish on sides. They have small ears concealed by fur, small eyes, and short tails darker on upper surface than on lower.

Active day and night. Feed on green plants, bulbs, nuts and fruits. Signs: surface runways beside logs and rocks, in moss etc. Nest beneath log or rock.

Found in damp pine forests and on tundra throughout Canada and in northern USA, further south in Allegheny and Rocky Mountain areas.

Southern Redback Voles: most widespread and found furthest south. Tundra Redback Voles: live in far north. Californian Redback Voles: found only in Pacific states and B.C.

80

Meadow Vole

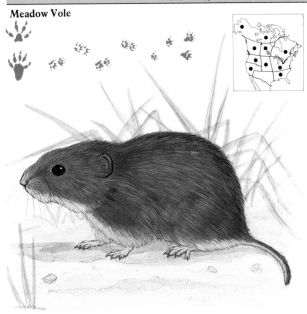

Small rodents, weighing up to 6oz., with long soft brownish or grayish, sometimes grizzled fur, lighter colored undersides, short ears concealed by fur and small eyes. They have relatively short tails, often darker above, lighter below.

Active day and night. Feed on green vegetation, like grasses, sedges and clovers and also on roots in winter. Signs: runways amongst the roots of the grasses together with piles of grass cuttings. Nest made of grass in burrow or above ground.

Many species; most found in grassy meadows in both lowlands and mountain areas. Others live in woodland or in tundra. Throughout most of N. America except the southwest.

Meadow Vole: found from northern Canada to central areas of USA. Mountain Vole: lives in mountain meadows of the Rockies. Woodland Vole: lives in woods in eastern and central USA.

MUSKRAT
10–12in.; tail 8–10in.

A medium-sized rodent, weighing 2–4lb., with dense, dark brown fur and longer guard hairs, becoming paler on the underside and silvery on the throat. Thick scaly tail flattened from side to side.

Mostly nocturnal. Feeds mainly on water plants as well as on frogs, crayfish and clams. Signs: makes large house up to 5ft. across and 4ft. high in mid water or in bank, with underwater entrances. Makes bank slides, runways and tunnels.

Found in ponds, marshes and slow-moving streams throughout most of N. America except parts of the south and north.

Florida Water Rat: smaller with round tail, lives in Florida.
Nutria: larger with round tail. **Beaver**: larger with tail flattened from top to bottom.

A very large rodent, weighing 30–60lb., with brown fur and a characteristic large black scaly tail, paddle-shaped and flattened from top to bottom, and large webbed hindfeet. It has obvious orange front teeth, small ears and small eyes.

Mostly nocturnal. Feeds on bark and twigs of trees like willow and aspen. Signs: Beaver lodges, houses of mud-caulked logs and twigs up to 6ft. high and 40ft. wide, log dams, gnawed stumps and trees. Slap of tail on water heard as Beaver dives.

Found in ponds, lakes and slow-moving streams throughout most of N. America except the far north, the southwest and Florida.

Muskrat: smaller with tail flattened from side to side. **Nutria**: also smaller with a round tail. **River Otter**: an elongated body and a furry tail.

A large rodent, weighing up to 30lb., with an arched, clumsy body and short legs and tail. The front of the body has long brown guard hairs and spines and there are quills on the rump and tail. The feet have characteristic "pebbly" soles.

Mainly nocturnal. Feed on green plants and on the inner bark of trees in winter; may kill the trees. A good climber. Den made in hollow tree or in rock crevice. Uses loosely attached quills in self defense as it swings its tail at predators.

Found in woodland and brush in much of Canada except the far north and in northeastern and north central USA. Often seen by the side of the highway, especially where salt has been used.

No similar species.

Water Vole (1)

Large vole (5½–6½in. plus 2in. tail) with gray-brown fur and lighter gray underside. It has a relatively long tail, darker above than beneath. This vole has a rather different lifestyle to most, for it lives near water and is a good swimmer. Burrows are made on banks of streams and marshes and connected to the water by wide runways. Feeds on water plants and willows. Found in foothills and mountains in western USA and Canada.

Florida Water Rat (2)

Medium-sized rodent (about 8in. plus 4–6in. tail), like a small Muskrat, covered in dense brown fur with longer guard hairs. It has a long round tail, sparsely covered in long hairs. Similar life style to a Muskrat, living in marshes and slow-moving streams. Builds houses in shallow water but they are no more than 2ft. across. Makes feeding platforms and feeds on water plants. Found in Florida and southern tip of Georgia.

OTHER RODENTS

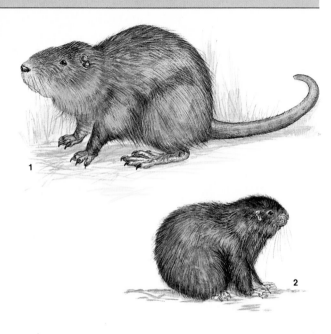

Nutria (1)

Large rodent (20–25in. plus 12–15in. tail) with brown fur, lighter on the underside, and a long round, sparsely hairy tail. Has webbed hind feet. Introduced from S. America for its fur and has become naturalized in many parts of the USA. It lives in marshes, streams and ponds, making burrows in the bank with the entrance above water. Has feeding station of logs and debris on shore, about 5ft. across, and feeds on water plants.

Mountain Beaver (2)

Relatively large rodent (12–17in. plus 1in. tail) with a blunt head like a marmot. It has dark brown fur, lighter on the underside, small ears and a tiny tail. It is found only on the west coast in Oregon, Calif. and B.C. where it lives in wet forest areas. Makes large burrows, indicated by mounds of earth, often beneath vegetation on banks of streams, and many runways. Feeds on grasses and ferns, as well as on bark of trees.

A small animal, like a guinea pig, with long gray-brown fur even on the soles of the feet, no visible tail and rounded prominent ears. These animals are very vocal, making a series of short high-pitched squeaks or whistles.

Active by day. Colonial. Feed on green plants and "hay", grasses and other plants which the pikas dry in heaps, turning the heaps to ensure even drying and moving them in rain. Hay is stored in burrows beneath rocks during rain and for winter.

Found on rockslides and steep rocky slopes near the timberline in the Rocky Mountains of Alberta, B.C. and western USA. May be seen in the mountain National Parks.

Collared Pika lives in Alaska and Mackenzie Mountains; it is very similar to the Pika but has a broad band of pale gray fur around its neck.

SNOWSHOE HARE
12–18in.

Hares have long hind legs, long ears and a small tail. Snowshoe Hares have brown fur in summer with a dusky tail and black-tipped ears; in winter the coat turns white except for black ear-tips. Soles of feet are furred, hence "snowshoes."

Nocturnal. Hares spend most of the daylight hours in a depression (or "form") in grass or other soft vegetation which becomes molded to their shape. Feed on green vegetation, buds, bark and berries depending on season, also on meat.

Found in forest areas throughout most of Canada except the extreme far north; also in Alaska and in northern areas of the USA, further south in mountain areas.

Arctic Hare: a large hare, gray-brown in summer but always has a white tail; found in far north of Canada. European Hare: large brown hare, top of tail black.

Large hare, weighing up to 7lb., with very long black-tipped ears and very long back legs. It has a gray-brown body with a white underside and a black stripe on the upper surface of its tail. It can leap away very quickly if threatened.

Active at night and at dusk and dawn. Spends the day in the form or in scrape under sagebrush. Feeds on green vegetation including alfalfa in summer, on dry plants in winter. Makes trail from feeding places to form. May be seen along highways.

Found in open prairies and more arid areas with sparse vegetation in western and central USA, but absent from Canada and northernmost areas of the States.

Whitetail Jackrabbit: has white tail, found in prairies and arid areas of northern states and southern Canada. **Antelope Jackrabbit**: white sides flash as it runs.

Quite large rabbit, weighing up to 4lb., with brownish or grayish fur and a white cottony tail. There is a reddish-brown patch of fur on the nape of the neck. The ears and hind legs are long but proportionately shorter than those of a hare.

Nocturnal and active early and late in the day. Feeds on green plants in the summer and can be a pest in gardens and on farm land, and on bark and twigs in winter when it can damage young trees.

Found in thickets and on the edges of woods, in cultivated areas and in brush in eastern and central USA as far west as Arizona in the south and N. Dakota in the north.

Desert Cottontail: smaller than Eastern Cottontail, has yellow gray fur. Nuttall's Cottontail: black-tipped ears, lives in sagebrush and upland areas in western USA.

90

Antelope Jackrabbit (1)
Similar to Blacktail Jackrabbit but with even longer ears and very long back legs. This hare has white sides and undersides which seem to flash as it makes huge leaps. Found in desert areas with sparse vegetation in southern Arizona and New Mexico.

Brush Rabbit (2)
Small brown rabbit, about 12in. long, with quite small dark ears and short hind legs and tail. Lives in brush in Pacific states of USA; may be seen in cities.

Desert Cottontail (3)
Similar to Eastern Cottontail but with grayer fur tinged with yellow, a rust-colored nape and longer ears. Lives in sparse grassland, arid areas and sagebrush in southwestern and western USA.

Swamp Rabbit (4)
Large rabbit, up to 17in. long, brownish-gray in color flecked with black, with whitish undersides and rust-colored feet. Lives in marshes and swamps in southeastern USA from Texas to Georgia. Good swimmer.

ELK OR WAPITI
4–5ft tall

A large deer with a reddish-brown coat, pale yellow-brown rump and a small light-colored tail. Males weigh up to 1000lb. and have large antlers in season (from summer to early spring); females are smaller, weigh up to 600lb. and have no antlers.

Most active early mornings and evenings. Feeds on lush grasses, lichens and leaves of bushes. Signs: mud wallows with the musky elk scent, broken branches, trees with bark stripped and also rubbed with strips of hanging velvet from antlers.

Found in grassland and mountain meadows and woods in summer, lower mountain slopes often in dense woodland in winter. Seen in National Parks in western USA and Canada.

Whitetail and **Mule Deer**: much smaller, weighing less than half as much as Elk. **Moose**: larger, over 6ft. tall, with a broad fleshy nose, a hanging dewlap and wide flat antlers.

92

MOOSE
5–6½ft. tall

The largest of all the deer worldwide, with a dark brown coat, a broad fleshy nose and a hanging dewlap beneath the chin. Males weigh up to 1100lb. and have broad flat antlers from summer to winter. Females are smaller with no antlers.

Most active at night but may be seen in early morning and evening. Browse on twigs and buds of willows and aspen and also feed on aquatic plants. Signs: mud wallows with moose scent, bark and twigs torn on trees.

Found in forest areas, especially near water and marshes, throughout Canada except the far north, in the Rocky Mountains and in the north east in the USA.

Elk: yellow-brown rump, no dewlap and no fleshy nose. **Mule** and **Whitetail Deer**: very much smaller, no fleshy nose.

MULE DEER
About 3ft. tall

These deer are reddish-brown in summer with whiter undersides, grayer on the back in winter. Males weigh up to 400lb. and have antlers in which the prongs divide equally. Females weigh up to 150lb. and have no antlers. Tail is black-tipped.

Mainly active at night, also in early morning and evening. Browse on a variety of shrubs, also on herbaceous plants. Signs: rubs on trees where males have marked territory with antlers, ripped vegetation, bed in leaves or snow.

Found in a variety of habitats from woodland to brush and grassland wherever browse plants are available, from western Canada to California as far east as Manitoba and Kansas.

Blacktail Deer: subspecies of Mule Deer with tails which are black on top, live on northwest Pacific coast. **Whitetail Deer**: tail not tipped with black, antlers have single main beam.

WHITETAIL DEER

About 3ft. tall

These deer are very similar in size and color to Mule Deer but can be readily distinguished from them by the white tail. The antlers of the males have a single forward-pointing beam with prongs borne unequally on it.

Mainly active at night, also in early morning and evening. Browse on twigs and leaves of conifers and other trees, also feed on acorns and nuts. Signs: rubs on trees where males have rubbed antlers, torn conifer shoots, bed in leaves or snow.

Found in woodland and brush as well as farmland and swamps, throughout the USA except the southwest, and in southern Canada.

Mule Deer: tail has black tip. Blacktail Deer: tail is black on top. **Elk**: much larger, yellow-brown rump.

CARIBOU
3–4ft. tall

Heavy-looking, brown deer with whitish mane and neck, whitish rump and ankles, large feet and hooves. Males and about half females have brown antlers, those of males much broader than females'. Males weigh up to 600lb., females half that.

Usually live in small groups in summer and winter; form large herds when they migrate in spring and fall. Browse on lichens, twigs and grasses. Signs: migration trails, torn shoots and lichens, rubs on trees where males have rubbed antlers, beds.

Found in coniferous forests in the southern parts of their range in winter, in woodland, muskeg and on the northern tundra in summer, across Canada.

Barren Ground Caribou: lighter in color, found further north, all Caribou are considered by many authorities to be same species.
Elk: yellow-brown rump, no forward prong on antlers.

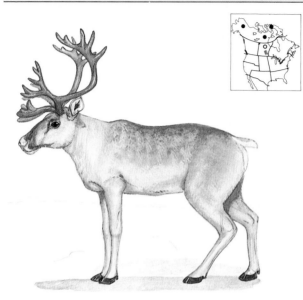

Northern Caribou are generally lighter in color, ranging from light brown to nearly white in far north of their range. They are generally smaller than members of the southern population, males weighing up to 400lb., females about half that.

Usually live in small groups within large herds, which are continually on the move. Feed on lichens, willow and mosses. Signs: migration trails, torn vegetation and lichens, rubs on bushes where males have rubbed antlers.

Found in coniferous forests in winter, migrate north to tundra in spring, spend summer on the tundra and migrate south to forests in late summer and fall.

Southern Caribou are generally darker in color and larger. Reindeer: have been introduced from northern Europe, are smaller, weighing up to 250lb.

PRONGHORN
3ft. tall

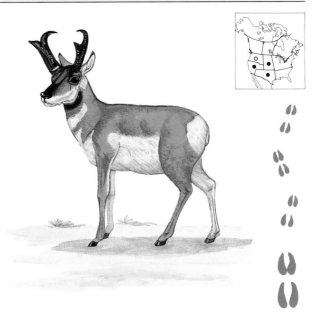

A deer-like animal, light reddish brown in color with white sides, underside and rump and white bands on the throat and sides of face. They weigh up to 130lb., but females are slightly smaller. Males have pronged horns, not antlers.

Live in small groups in summer, in larger herds in winter, always on the move. Browse on grasses, cacti and sagebrush. Pronghorns are the fastest animals in N. America, bounding over the ground at up to 70mph for short distances.

Found in open prairies and sagebrush areas in southwestern, western and central USA as far north as southern Saskatchewan.

White markings on rump, sides and face distinguish Pronghorn from Deer, as do the horns instead of antlers on the males.

MOUNTAIN GOAT
About 3ft. tall

These goats have thick whitish-yellow hair, longer in winter than in summer. Males are slightly larger than females but both sexes have smooth, black, more or less straight horns. Males have a "beard," an extension of the mane below the chin.

Most active in early morning and evening. Feed on grasses, sedges and other alpine plants in summer, on lichens, mosses and woody shoots in winter. May be seen in small groups on ledges in western Canadian mountain National Parks.

Found on steep mountain slopes and ledges around the timberline, but higher in summer than in winter, in the mountains of western Canada and north western USA.

Bighorn Sheep: males have large, heavy, brownish, curved horns; horns of females similar in form but much smaller. **Dall Sheep**: similar horns to Bighorn Sheep but yellowish.

BIGHORN SHEEP
About 3ft. tall

These sheep have short brown or grayish-brown hair with a whitish rump and nose. The underside and backs of the legs are also whitish. Males have large brown, curved horns, females much smaller horns. The horns show concentric growth rings.

Active during the day. Live in small groups, rams and ewes separate. Feed on grasses and sedges in summer, woody shoots in winter. Signs: beds smelling of urine and with droppings around, grayish-brown hair caught on rocks and trees.

Found in alpine meadows and on rocky slopes, higher in summer than in winter, in undisturbed areas in mountains of western USA and southwestern Canada: best seen in some National Parks.

Dall Sheep: white or gray-haired (sometimes black), live in northwestern Canada and Alaska. **Mountain Goat**: white-haired with straight black horns.

100

These sheep have short hair and are whitish in color, often tinged with yellow or gray. Males bear large, curved, yellowish horns; females have much smaller horns. Horns have concentric growth rings.

Active during the day. Live in small groups in summer, ewes and rams separate, together in winter. Feed on woody plants like willow, cranberries and sage. Signs: beds like those of Bighorn Sheep, white hair caught on rocks and bushes.

Found on rocky mountain slopes in Alaska, the Yukon and northern B.C.

Fannin and Stone Sheep are gray and black-backed forms of Dall Sheep which occur in the south of their range. **Bighorn Sheep**: brown hair. **Mountain Goat**: straight black horns and long hair.

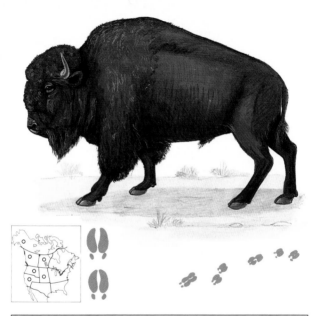

A very large animal, weighing up to 2000lb., with a massive head, a large hump on the shoulders and long shaggy hair forming a mane and on the legs. There is also a tuft of hair on the tail. Both sexes have short, black, curving horns.

Active during the day, particularly in early morning and evening. Live in large herds. Graze mainly on grasses and sedges. Signs: dust wallows, trampled ground and bark rubbed away on trees.

Only relatively few are left of these once numerous animals that roamed the prairies. May be seen in some of the National Parks in central and western USA and Canada.

No similar species.

MUSKOX
4–5ft. tall

A large animal, weighing up to 900lb., with a massive head and shoulder hump. It has brown shaggy hair hanging almost to its feet. The horns are distinctive — from the center of the forehead they curve forwards and end in pointed tips.

Active during the day. Live mostly in small groups. Graze on grasses and sedges in summer, on woody shoots in winter. Signs: distinctive musky scent can be detected some distance away.

Found on the tundra in northern Canada, in lowland areas in the summer, on exposed slopes in winter where the wind blows the snow away to expose the underlying vegetation.

No similar species.

PECCARY
2ft. tall

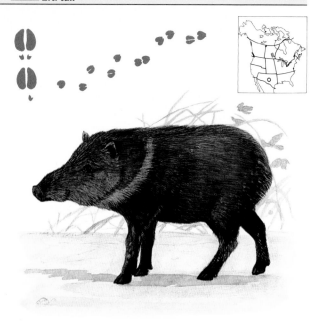

A pig-like animal, weighing up to 50lb., with coarse, grizzled black hair and a "collar" of lighter hair over the shoulders. It has a pig-like snout with more or less straight tusks in the upper jaws, and no visible tail.

Active mainly in early morning and evening in small herds, avoiding the midday heat. Feed mainly on Prickly Pear and other cacti, also on mesquite and other plants, acorns when available. Signs: torn cacti, trampled and torn up ground.

Found in arid desert country with sparse vegetation and in brush, near water holes, in southern areas of Arizona, New Mexico and Texas.

Wild Boar: introduced from Europe and now wild in many southern states; they are larger than peccaries and the tusks curve upwards. They have long straight tails.

A massive, sluggish animal with a dark, leathery hide over a thick layer of blubber. The head is broad with thick cleft lips and whiskers on the muzzle. The forelegs form paddles, hind legs are absent, the tail is a horizontal rounded fluke.

Rest and browse underwater during the day, feeding on aquatic plants like water hyacinths and water lilies. Can remain submerged for about 15mins. Live in small groups and now protected as numbers have declined in recent years.

Found in warm coastal waters, especially in lagoons, river mouths and bays on the Gulf of Mexico and north along the southern Atlantic coast to N. Carolina.

No similar species.

CALIFORNIAN SEA LION
♂ up to 8ft.; ♀ up to 6ft.

Streamlined body with limbs forming flippers. Hind flippers are turned forward when animal walks on land. These sea lions are brown in color, with small ears and males "bark" almost continually. Males weigh up to 600lb., females only 200lb.

Rests and sleeps in large herds on land during the day, hunts at sea during night. Feeds on fishes, octopus and squid. Familiar to visitors to zoos and circuses as "seals." Signs: barking of males as they defend their territories.

Found along the Pacific coast, mostly on rocky beaches and islands, from the Gulf of California north to B.C., but much more common in southern part of range. Protected.

Northern Sea Lion: yellow-brown, larger, males weigh up to 2000lb., with enlarged neck and shoulders. **Alaska Fur Seal**: smaller, males have enlarged neck and shoulders, grayish mane.

ALASKA FUR SEAL
♂ up to 6ft.; ♀ up to 4½ft.

Streamlined body with small head and ears and large flippers.
Hind flippers are turned forward when animal walks on land.
Males weigh up to 600lb., almost black with enlarged neck and
shoulders and a gray mane. Females weigh up to 120lb., gray.

Live in harem groups during the breeding season in summer, with
a dominant male and up to 50 females. Young bachelor males live
in herds outside breeding grounds. Spend rest of year at sea. Feed
on various fishes and squid.

Found on Pacific coast from the Bering Sea to California but more
common in northern part of their range. Breeding herds gather on
rocky island beaches, especially on Pribilof Is.

Northern Sea Lion: much larger, yellow-brown in color.

WALRUS
♂ up to 12ft.; ♀ up to 9ft.

Very large seal with characteristic white tusks present in both sexes, but larger in the male than in the female. Male weighs up to 2800lb., female up to 1800lb. Hind flippers turn forward on land. Muzzle has many stiff whiskers.

Live a nomadic existence, resting by day in groups on pack ice or islands. Feed on the bottom in shallow water, using tusks to dig for clams, whelks, worms, sea-cucumbers etc. Signs: very noisy animals, bellowing can be heard up to a mile away.

Found on islands and on pack ice in Arctic Ocean, in north Atlantic south to Hudson Bay and north Pacific on northwest coast of Alaska.

No other comparable seal. Tusks and size make Walruses immediately recognizable.

ELEPHANT SEAL

♂ up to 20ft.; ♀ about 10ft.

Very large seal, adult male weighs over 7500lb., female up to
1800lb. Body covered in rough hide, hind flippers are turned
backwards and male has a large snout overhanging the muzzle.
Color varies from pale brown to gray.

Rest by day in herds on sandy beaches and feed at night on squid,
sharks and rays. Spend fall months at sea. Numbers now
recovering slowly from massive decline during hunting in
nineteenth century.

Found on the Pacific coast on sandy beaches of offshore islands
and on the mainland, from Baja California to B.C., but only
commonly seen in south of range.

All other seals are much smaller. **Sea Lion** and **Fur Seal**: hind
flippers turn forwards. **Harbor Seal**: spotted.

HARBOR SEAL
5–6ft.

Streamlined body with hind flippers turned backwards. Color varies from gray to brown with dark spots on the back, creamy white with spots on the underside. These seals are quite small, weighing about 250lb., and have no visible ears.

Spend a lot of their time basking on shore in groups or hunting fishes which they may follow up-river with the tide. They bark when disturbed and enter the water. They cannot move as easily on land as Sea Lions and Fur Seals.

Found in river mouths, harbors and on sandbanks in coastal waters, on Atlantic, Arctic and Pacific coasts and in Hudson Bay.

Most other seals are found further north and out at sea. Gray Seal: quite rare, larger, lives in sea from coast of Labrador to New England. **Sea Lions**: hind flippers turned forwards.

Similar in form to the Harbor Seal but with a light gray body and black markings. Males often have a black "saddle" on the back, females less regular markings. Males weigh up to 400lb., females are slightly smaller.

These are the seals culled in the annual seal hunt off the Canadian coast. They congregate there on drifting pack ice to give birth to their pups in February. Feed on small fish and larger crustaceans.

Found on pack ice and out at sea in the Arctic and Atlantic Oceans for much of the year, spending the winter in Labrador waters on the ice or in the sea.

Other Arctic seals include Ringed Seal: smallest of the seals, color variable often marbled with spots and streaks. Bearded Seal: characteristic tuft of whiskers on each side of muzzle.

COMMON DOLPHIN

6–8½ft.

Sleek, streamlined animal with a dark gray back, very light gray underside and a pattern of yellow and gray streaks on the sides. Also dark "spectacles" over the eyes. It has a "beak" about 6in. long, and black pointed flippers.

Seen in large groups swimming, rolling and leaping in the sea, or riding bow waves of ships. Feed on fishes like sardines and herring, also on squid. May be seen in marine aquaria and zoos.

Found in temperate and warm waters of the Atlantic and Pacific Oceans some distance from the coast.

Pacific Common Dolphin: considered by some authorities to belong to different species, slimmer and lacks gray streaks on sides. White-sided Dolphin: white stripe along each side.

Sleek, streamlined animal, generally light gray all over but slightly paler on the underside than on the back. A large dolphin, recognizable by its size, color, high dorsal fin and the groove that separates its 3in. beak from its forehead.

Seen in small groups swimming and rolling in the sea, usually with just the back and dorsal fin showing, or riding bow waves of ships. Feed on a variety of different fishes. This is the dolphin that usually performs in dolphinaria.

Found in temperate and warm areas of the Atlantic and Pacific Oceans, usually in coastal waters quite close to the shore.

Spotted Dolphin: smaller and slimmer with spots all over body and long, white-tipped beak.

HARBOR PORPOISE
4–6ft.

Streamlined but quite thick-bodied, with a blunt snout and no beak. It has a black back, black flippers and fluke and a white underside, with a bluish-gray patch on each side. The dorsal fin is low and the flippers are small and oval.

Seen in small groups in inshore waters, river mouths and harbors, feeding on fishes like mackerel and herring, but much less tame than dolphins. May become tangled in fishing nets. Numbers have declined in recent years.

Found in shallow coastal waters of northern Atlantic and Pacific Oceans, as far south as the Delaware River and California.

Dolphins have beaks.

A distinctive whale, with a black back and a white underside with a white process extending backwards onto each side behind the fin. It also has a white eye patch. Male has very long dorsal fin (up to 6ft. long), but that of female is shorter.

Nomads, seen in extended family groups of up to 40 members. They are hunters, taking seals, sharks and other fishes, small whales and porpoises but are not dangerous to man. May be seen in some marine aquaria.

Found in inshore waters and in the open ocean, most often in cool but not icy water, in both the Atlantic and Pacific Oceans.

False Killer Whale: black all over with small curved dorsal fin.

SPERM WHALE
35–50ft.

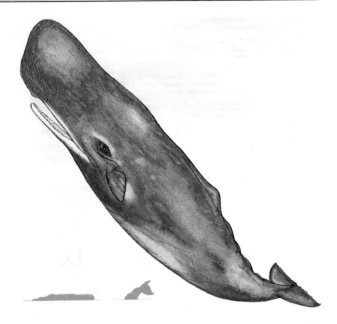

The huge blunt head of this large whale, together with its small lower jaw makes it easily recognizable. It is a dark bluish gray in color, has small flippers and no true dorsal fin, only a series of "humps." Females are smaller than males.

Live in groups of 30 or more, either females and calves or young males together. Characteristic left-handed spout blows at 45°. Feed on deep water animals, giant squid and fishes. Numbers have declined seriously from pressure of hunting.

Found in Atlantic and Pacific Oceans, males in cool waters in summer while females and calves remain in warmer areas. Most often seen where ocean currents meet.

Humpback Whale: different shape, long whitish flippers and expanding vertical spout.

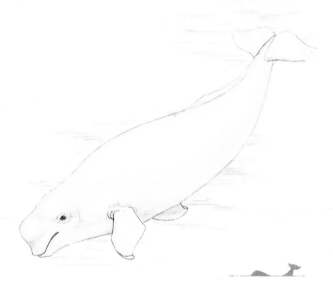

A distinctive small whale, white all over, with a rounded head and body, flippers with upturned tips and no dorsal fin. Calves are blue gray.

Live in small groups of females and calves or young males together, but migrate in much larger herds. Feed at the bottom in shallow water, rivers and estuaries of Arctic Ocean on shrimps, crabs and fishes.

Found in Arctic, northern Pacific and Atlantic Oceans and in Hudson Bay. They migrate from summer feeding grounds in the far north, south as far as Connecticut or B.C. in the winter.

No similar species.

117

HUMPBACK WHALE
About 50ft.

A large black-backed whale, with tubercles on its head, grooves on its whitish throat and breast, long mottled white flippers with serrated front edges and a small dorsal fin set on a fleshy platform two thirds of the way along the body.

Live in small family groups linked to other more distant groups by the "songs" of the whales. Characteristic spout is a vertical expanding cloud of spray. Feed on krill and shoals of fishes. Probably no more than 5000 of these whales left.

Found in Atlantic and Pacific Oceans. They migrate between summer feeding grounds in the far north and winter breeding grounds near Hawaii, off Baja California and the West Indies.

Rorqual: does not raise the fluke before diving as the Humpback does, small dark flippers. Fin Whale: flat-headed whale, longer and slimmer in shape.

118

The largest animal ever known. A long, streamlined whale with a dark blue-gray back, lighter tips to the flippers and lighter underside, and long grooves on its throat. Its dorsal fin is small and set well back.

Live in small groups. Spout is a single tall column of spray. Feed in surface waters, straining planktonic crustaceans from the water with the baleen plates. Hunting has resulted in drastic reduction in numbers, about 10,000 left in the world.

Most found in southern hemisphere but a few live in Pacific and Atlantic Oceans. These migrate north to feed in the Arctic Ocean in summer, migrating towards the equator for the winter.

Fin Whale: smaller, grayer, does not show fluke when diving.

A distinctive large whale, mottled gray in color and covered with large clusters of barnacles. It has a bowed head and no dorsal fin, instead there are a series of small humps at the rear of the back.

Mostly solitary. In the Arctic, whales feed at the bottom, stirring up the mud and filtering off the shrimps. Can be seen in Californian lagoons and off the west coast as they migrate in large herds. About 11,000 left in east Pacific.

Found in Arctic and off the Pacific coast. They migrate from summer feeding grounds in the far north to winter in breeding grounds in lagoons on coast of Baja California.

Sperm Whale: much bigger head, dark gray in color.

A large black whale, with a characteristic shape. The body is smooth without any dorsal fin or humps on the back and the upper jaw is arched for the suspension of baleen plates used in feeding. There are lumpy patches of barnacles on the head.

Solitary or in small groups. Spout is distinctive, producing a V-shape from two separate blowholes. Feed by swimming slowly in surface waters and straining off planktonic crustaceans in the baleen plates. Probably about 2000 left in the world.

At one time this was the "common" whale, found throughout the north Atlantic and north Pacific. Small populations remain in shallow waters off the Aleutians and the coast of Alaska.

Bowhead Whale: upper jaw even more highly arched, no patches of barnacles on head, white chin.

Index and check-list

All species in roman type are illustrated
Keep a record of your sightings by checking the boxes